3. plus cyan blue ink

4. plus black ink

First Published in 1971 by
Macdonald and Company
(Publishers) Limited
St. Giles House
49-50 Poland Street
London W1

Chief Editor
Sandie Oram M.A.
Illustrator:
Kenneth Ody

Second impression 1973
ISBN 0 356 03785 1
MFL 33

Made and printed in Great Britain
by A. Wheaton & Company
Exeter Devon

MACDONALD FIRST LIBRARY

Light and Colour

Macdonald Educational
49-50 Poland Street
London W1

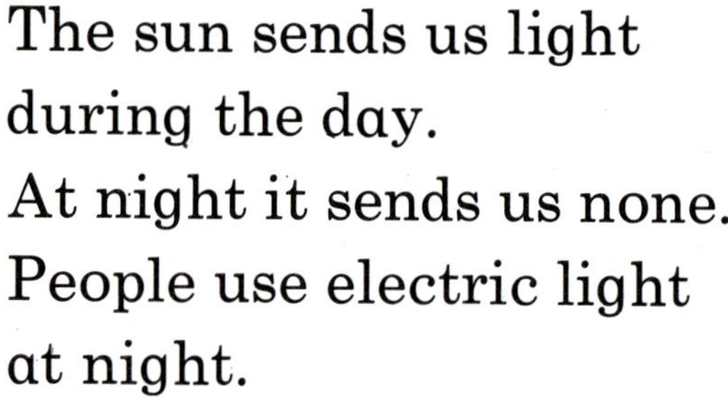

The sun sends us light during the day. At night it sends us none. People use electric light at night.

Nobody can see anything without light. You can see things only when light is shining onto them. The light shines onto things and bounces off them into your eyes. This is how you see things.

At night you can see the moon.
It shines brightly and sends out light.
But the moon does not make light.
The light of the moon is really the
light of the sun shining onto it.
The sunlight bounces off the moon
towards the earth.
This is how you can see the moon.

Throw a stone into a pond.
It will send waves out in a circle.
Rays of light from the sun travel in waves like this.

Point a torch at the ceiling.
The light will travel straight up to the ceiling.
A ray of light travels in a straight line.

Some things can bend rays of light.
Light goes straight through glass and water.
But if the light hits them sideways glass and water bend light.

See how the pencil looks bent where it meets the water.
This is called 'refraction'.

Light goes through glass.
Windows are made of glass.
Everything can be seen
through this glass window.
It is 'transparent' glass.

Some glass lets in light,
but nothing can be seen
through it.
It is 'translucent' glass.

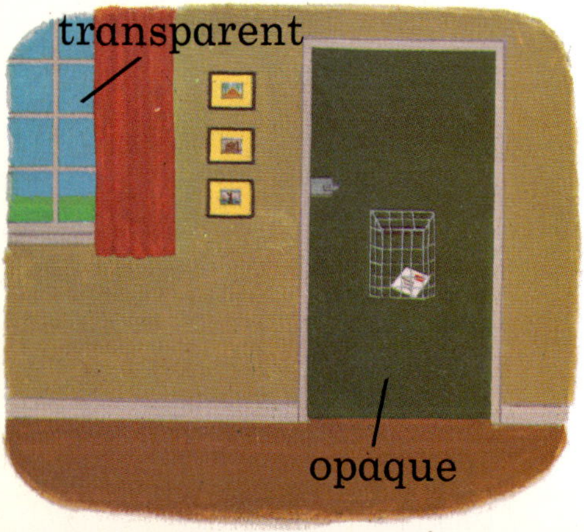

Light cannot go through
bricks or wood or other
solid things.
The door and wall stop
the light coming through.
Things which stop light
are called 'opaque'.

transparent

opaque

A mirror stops light and bounces, or 'reflects', it back.
The picture in a mirror is a reflection.
A reflection is the opposite way round.

Shiny things reflect light too.
The light hits the van from the side.
The van reflects the light in the opposite direction.

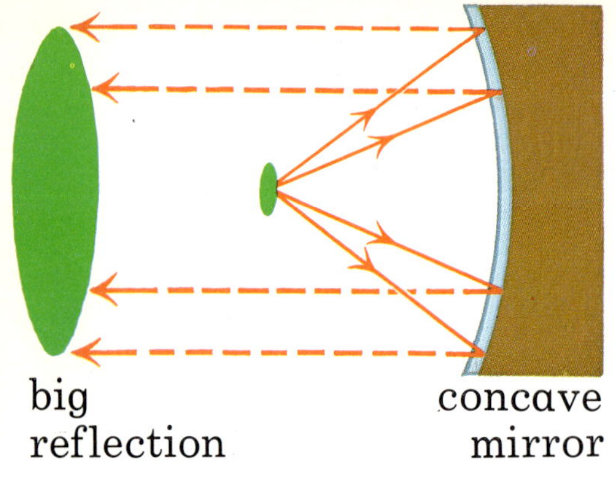

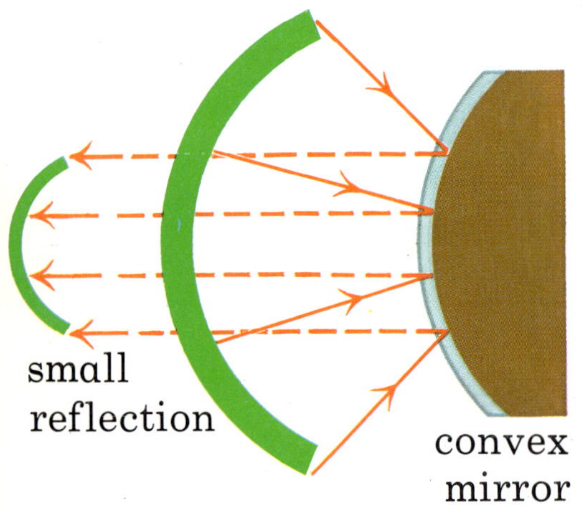

Some mirrors are curved. A 'concave' mirror curves inwards like the inside of a bowl. It takes in light from something small. It sends out a big big reflection.

A 'convex' mirror curves outwards like the outside of a bowl. It takes in light from a big area and sends out a smaller reflection. A convex driving mirror shows a small picture of a lot of the road.

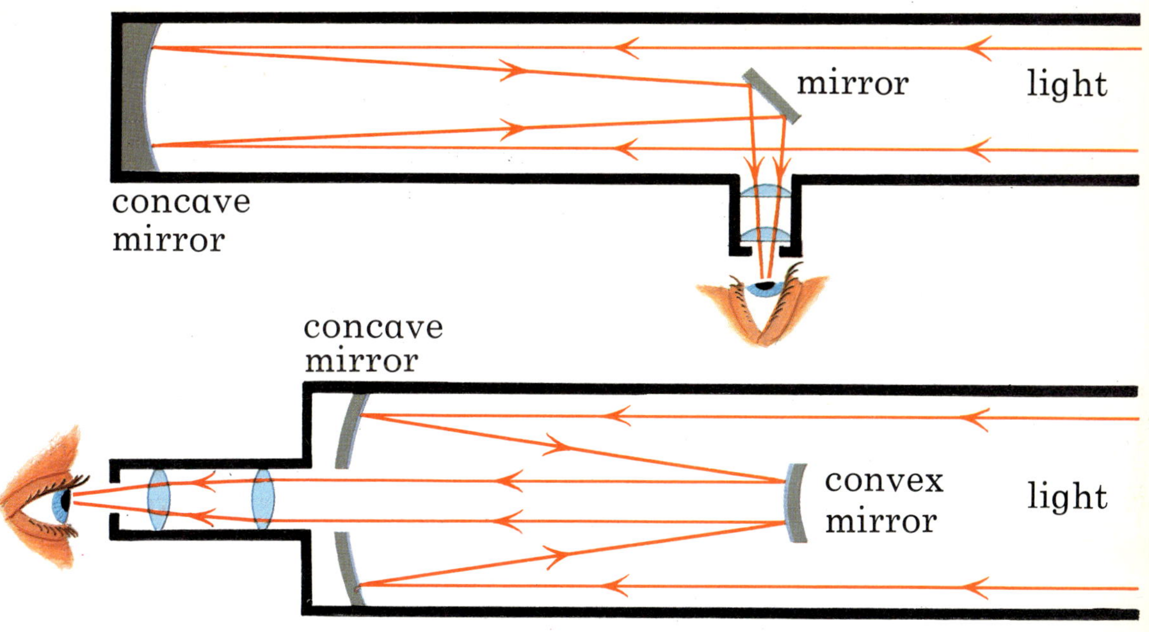

Telescopes are used to make far-away things look closer.

Light enters the telescope at one end.
It hits a concave mirror at the other end.
The concave mirror reflects the light back onto another mirror.
Then the light is reflected out to the eye.

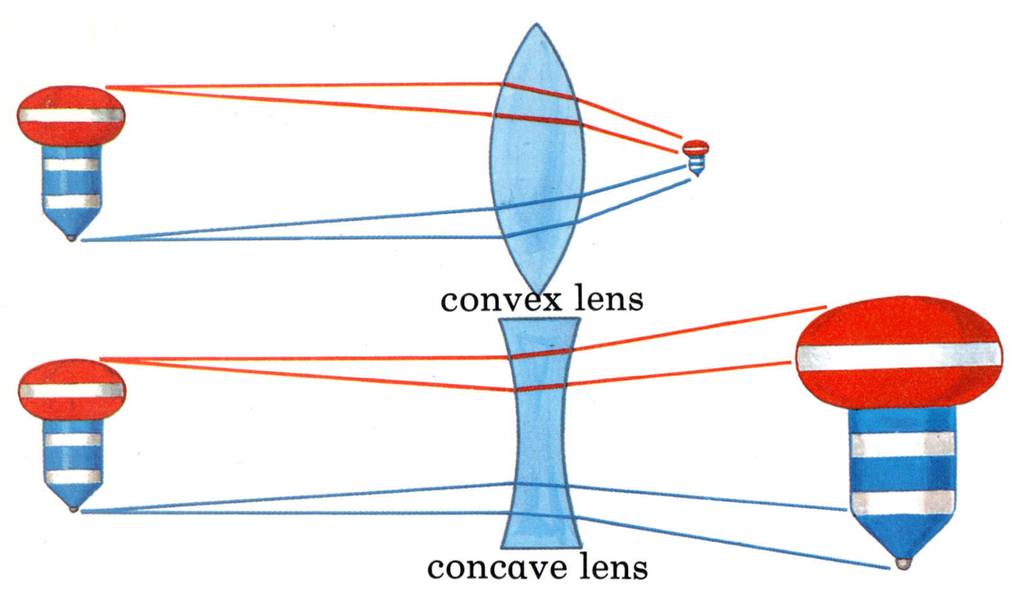

A ‘lens’ is a piece of glass.

There are concave and convex lenses.
Things can look bigger through concave lenses.
Through convex lenses things can look smaller.

The curved glass bends, or refracts, the light in a new direction.

Spectacles have lenses to help people see better.
A magnifying glass has a lens.
It makes things look big.

Cameras have lenses.
Some cameras have many different lenses.

camera

camera's lenses

Light looks white.
But white light is made from seven colours.
The seven colours are called the 'spectrum'.
Shine light through a 'prism' lens.
It will break the light into a spectrum.

The colours of the spectrum are red, orange, yellow, green, blue, indigo and violet.

Paint a cardboard circle
with all the colours of
the spectrum.
Put a pencil through the
middle of the circle.

Spin the pencil
round fast.
The painted circle will
look white.

A rainbow is a spectrum in the sky.
A rainbow is made by sunlight shining onto raindrops.
The raindrops are like prisms.
They break up the sunlight into the colours of the spectrum.

Coloured light rays can be seen. Other light rays cannot be seen. Ultra-violet rays lie at the violet edge of the spectrum. Ultra-violet rays turn skin brown.

Beside red rays are infra-red rays. Infra-red rays are hot. They can be used with a special camera. Then the camera can take photographs in the dark or in fog without needing bright lights.

badger at night

Something red looks red because it reflects the red from the spectrum. It soaks up, or absorbs, all the other colours. So only the colour red reaches your eyes.

Purple is a mixture of red and blue colours. Something purple reflects the red and blue colours of the spectrum. It absorbs the other colours.

White things reflect back all the seven colours which make white light.

Rays of sunlight are hot.
White cloth reflects back all the hot rays.
People in hot countries wear white clothes to keep them cool.

Red, green and blue are the most important colours of light. They are called 'primary' colours. Primary colours can be mixed to make any other colour.

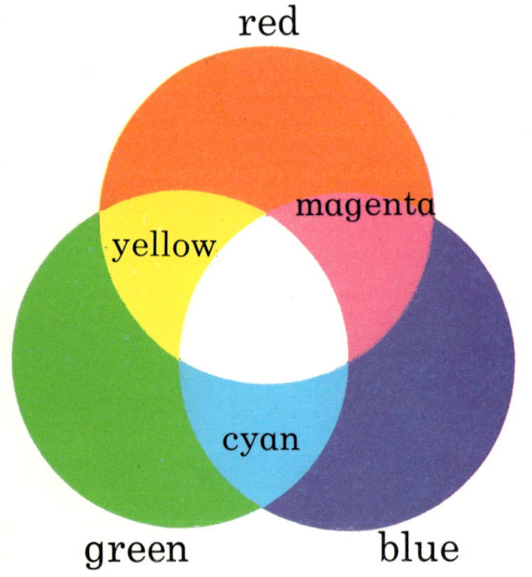

Green and blue light mixed make a greeny blue called 'cyan' blue. Blue and red light mixed make another red called 'magenta'. Red, green and blue light mixed together make white light.

A red light makes the clown look red.

Red and green light mixed make yellow light. In red and green light the clown is yellow.

The primary colours of light make white. In red, green and blue lights the clown looks white again.

The primary colours of paint are not the same as those of light.
The primary colours of paint are yellow, cyan blue and magenta red.

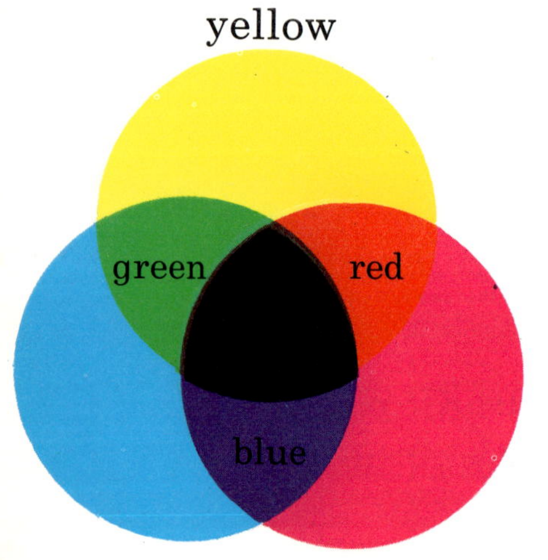

Yellow, cyan blue and magenta red paints can be mixed to make all other colours of paint.
Magenta and yellow make red.
The three colours together make black paint.

The painter wants to paint the door green.
He has no green paint.
But he has the primary colours of paint.
He can make any colour with them.
He mixes the cyan and yellow paints.
Now he has green paint.
If he mixed all three tins together he would make black paint.

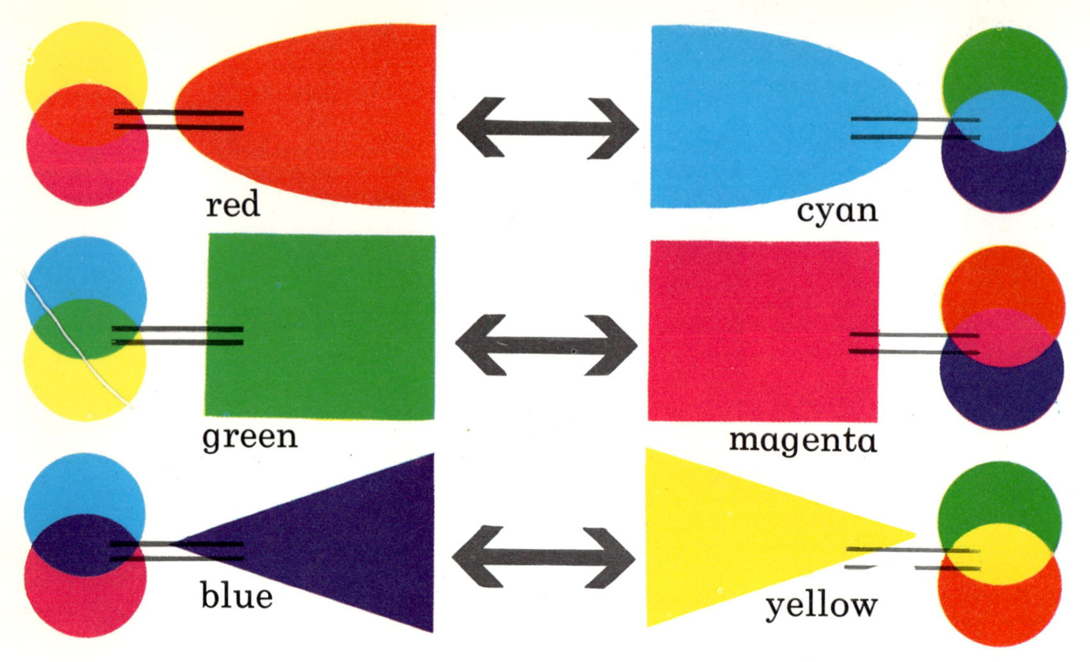

Blue and yellow are called
'complementary' colours.
Blue is made by cyan and magenta.
Yellow is made by green and red.
So a pair of complementary colours is made
by the other four primary colours.
A pair of complementary colours uses all
the six primary colours.

All the colours of light make white light. Blue and yellow light use all the other colours. Blue and yellow light mixed make white light.

All the colours of paint make black paint. Green and magenta paint use all the other colours. Green and magenta paint mixed make black paint.

Long ago men found out
how to make a few
colours from rocks
and plants.
They used these colours
to paint pictures.

The first pictures were
painted on the walls
of caves.

They made paints to colour their clothes. These paints are called 'dyes'. Cloth was dyed in big tubs. Today there are big machines for dyeing cloth.

Now dyes are made from coal tar.

Plants could make only a few colours of dye. Every kind of colour can be made with coal tar.

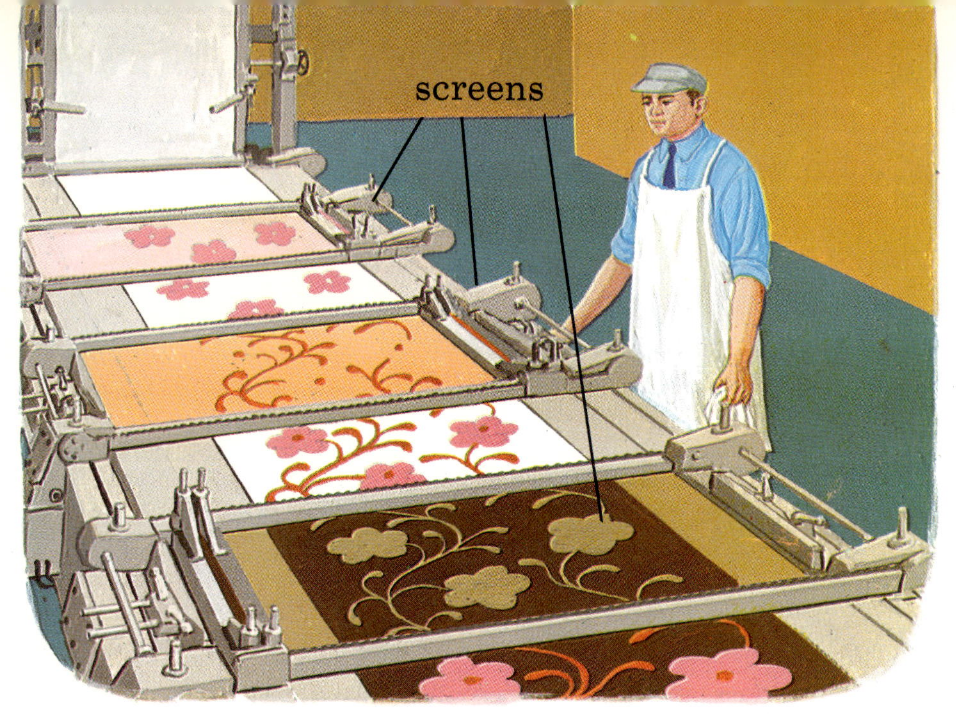

Coloured patterns can be printed onto cloth.
There are many ways of doing this.
One way is called 'screen printing'.
A screen has silk stretched over it.
The screens are part of a big machine.

Each screen has one
colour of the pattern.
Each screen prints only
one colour of dye.

The screens print the
parts of the pattern
on top of each other.

In the end the cloth
has one many-coloured
pattern.

Most people use electric light at home.
The light comes from an electric light bulb.
The bulb is made of glass.
Inside there is a thin wire called a filament.
Electricity makes the filament so hot that it shines.
The bulb is filled with special gas.
The gas stops the filament from burning away.

Street lights are very bright.
They are called 'discharge lamps'.
They are filled with gas.
Electricity makes the gas glow brightly.

In kitchens people often have discharge lamps called strip lighting.
These lights use ultra-violet rays.
They give a bright light like daylight.

glow-worm

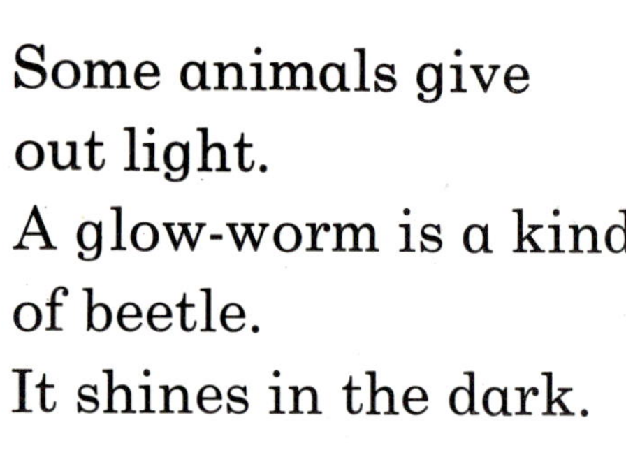

Some animals give
out light.
A glow-worm is a kind
of beetle.
It shines in the dark.

Other plants and rocks
can give out light.
This light is called
'phosphorescence'.
Phosphorescent light
shines but it is not
hot like other light.

Colour is very important in nature.
Many animals and insects have colours to match the places where they live.

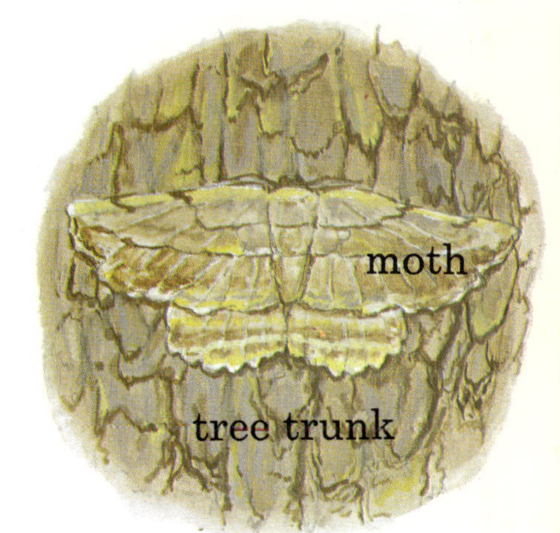

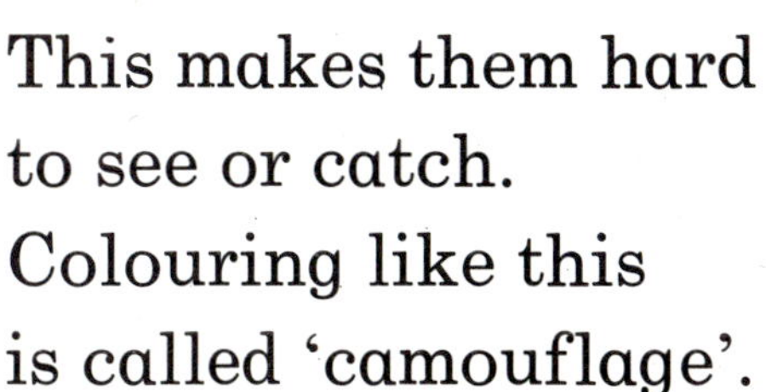
This makes them hard to see or catch.
Colouring like this is called ‘camouflage’.

The chameleon can change its colours to camouflage itself.
It looks brown next to mud and green next to leaves.

Index

MACDONALD FIRST LIBRARY

1 Prehistoric Animals
2 The Airline Pilot
3 Into Space
4 Knights and Castles
5 The Postman
6 Insects That Live Together
7 By the Sea
8 How Flowers Live
9 Water
10 Number
11 Shape
12 Sounds and Music
13 Cats
14 Frogs and Toads
15 Mushrooms and Toadstools
16 The Policeman
17 Under the Sea
18 Ships of Long Ago
19 Air
20 Cold Lands
21 Spiders
22 Pirates and Buccaneers
23 Size
24 Fire
25 Weather
26 Deserts
27 Skyscrapers
28 Monkeys and Apes
29 Trains and Railways
30 Trees and Wood
31 Cowboys
32 Time and Clocks
33 Light and Colour
34 Birds and Migration
35 The Universe
36 Farms and Farmers
37 Rocks and Mining
38 Rivers and River Life
39 Snakes and Lizards
40 Roads and Motorways
41 Ports and Harbours
42 Bridges and Tunnels
43 Towns and Cities
44 Horses and Ponies
45 Aeroplanes and Balloons
46 The Story of Cars
47 Mountains
48 Electricity
49 Television
50 Photography
51 The Jungle
52 The Dog Family
53 Gypsies and Nomads
54 Ballet and Dance
55 Paper and Printing
56 Food and Drink
57 Cloth and Weaving
58 Lakes and Dams
59 Building
60 Butterflies and Moths
61 Vanishing Animals
62 Animals that Burrow
63 Fuel and Energy
64 Animals with Shells
65 The Theatre
66 Health and Disease
67 Pollution
68 The Cinema
69 Signals and Messages
70 Fishing

How a colour book is printed

1. yellow ink

2. plus magenta red ink